NO QUIZ

Unlikely Pairs

FUN WITH FAMOUS WORKS OF ART

BOB RACZKA

M Millbrook Press · Minneapolis

To Mom and Dad—
Thanks for everything

Copyright © 2006 by Bob Raczka

Library of Congress Cataloging-
in-Publication Data
Raczka, Bob.
Unlikely pairs: fun with famous
works of art/Bob Raczka.
p. cm.
Summary: Invites the reader to discover
thirteen funny stories produced by pairing
twenty-six paintings from
different eras and styles.
ISBN-13: 978–0–7613–2936–7 (lib. bdg.)
ISBN-10: 0–7613–2936–6 (lib. bdg.)

1. Art appreciation—Juvenile literature.
[1. Art appreciation.
2. Painting.] I. Title.
N7477 .R34 2006
750'.1'1—dc22
2003014078

Designed by Tania Garcia
Picture Research by Pam Szen

Millbrook Press
A division of Lerner Publishing Group
241 First Avenue North
Minneapolis, MN 55401 U.S.A.

Website address: www.lernerbooks.com

Manufactured in the
United States of America
1 2 3 4 5 6 — DP — 11 10 09 08 07 06

Introduction

Whatever kind of art you like to look at when you go to a museum or gallery, chances are you focus on one piece at a time. After all, that's the way artists intend for their work to be appreciated.

But what if you looked at art in a new way—say, two pieces at a time?

On the following pages, I've divided 26 famous works of art into 13 "unlikely pairs." I call them unlikely because the works in each pair were either done by artists from completely different eras, or they were done in completely different styles. Seeing them together in an exhibit would be highly unlikely!

As you'll see, when you look at two very different pieces of art as a pair, your mind automatically starts making connections between them. Each pair seems to tell a funny story, and it's up to you to figure out what that story is.

But looking at art this way is more than fun. It can also change the way you feel about individual pieces and, hopefully, make you appreciate them even more. Who knows? It might even inspire you to create some "unlikely pairs" of your own.

Now, imagine you're walking through an art museum and you see the following works side by side…

Bob Raczka

Untitled

Keith Haring ◆ 1988 ◆ Owned by Estate of Keith Haring

The Guitar Player
Jan Vermeer ◆ 1672 ◆ Kenwood House, London, England

Soap Bubbles

Jean-Baptiste Siméon-Chardin ◆ c. 1733–34 ◆ National Gallery of Art, Washington, D.C.

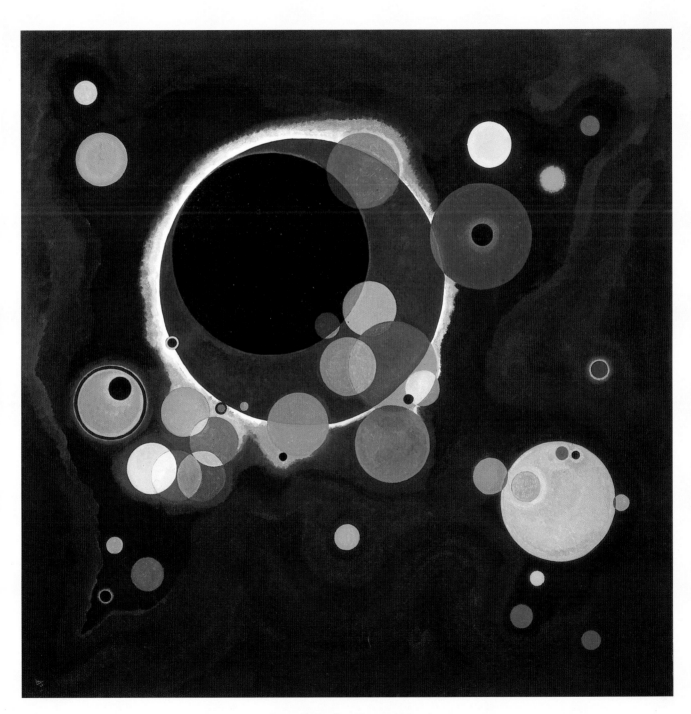

Several Circles (Einige Kreise)
Vasily Kandinsky ◆ 1926 ◆ The Solomon R. Guggenheim Museum, New York

Herakles Archer
Émile-Antoine Bourdelle ◆ 1909 ◆ Galerie Daniel Malingue, Paris, France

Target with Four Faces

Jasper Johns ◆ 1955 ◆ The Museum of Modern Art, New York, NY

Breezing Up (A Fair Wind)

Winslow Homer ◆ 1873–76 ◆ National Gallery of Art, Washington, D.C.

Spray

Roy Lichtenstein ◆ 1962 ◆ Private Collection

Floor Burger

Claes Oldenburg ◆ 1962 ◆ Art Gallery of Ontario, Toronto, Canada

The Cow with the Subtile Nose
Jean Dubuffet ◆ 1954 ◆ The Museum of Modern Art, New York

Loge with the Gilt Mask (La Loge au Mascaron Dore)
Henri de Toulouse-Lautrec ◆ 1893 ◆ National Gallery of Art, Washington, D.C.

The Ballet from "Robert le Diable"
Edgar Degas ◆ 1872 ◆ Metropolitan Museum of Art, New York

Do-It-Yourself Landscape
Andy Warhol ◆ 1962 ◆ Museum Ludwig, Cologne, Germany

Self-Portrait
Jean-Frédéric Bazille ◆ 1865 ◆ The Art Institute of Chicago, Chicago, Illinois

Spatial Concept, Expectations (Concetto Spaziale, Attesse)
Lucio Fontana ◆ 1959 ◆ The Solomon R. Guggenheim Museum, New York

Officer of the Imperial Guard on Horseback
Théodore Géricault ◆ 1812 ◆ Musée du Louvre, Paris, France

A Pair of Boots

Vincent van Gogh ◆ 1887 ◆ The Baltimore Museum of Art, Baltimore, Maryland

Captain Thomas Lee
Marcus Gheerhaerts the Younger ◆ 1594 ◆ Tate Gallery, London, England

The Thinker
Auguste Rodin ◆ 1879–89 ◆ The Cleveland Museum of Art, Cleveland, Ohio

Large Chess Board
Paul Klee ◆ 1937 ◆ Kunsthaus, Zurich, Switzerland

Niagara
Frederic Edwin Church ◆ 1857 ◆ The Corcoran Gallery of Art, Washington, D.C.

Fur Traders Descending the Missouri
George Caleb Bingham ◆ c. 1845 ◆ The Metropolitan Museum of Art, New York

Young Man Holding a Skull (Vanitas)
Frans Hals ◆ 1626–28 ◆ The National Gallery, London, England

The Scream
Edvard Munch ◆ 1893 ◆ National Gallery, Oslo, Norway

Keith Haring (1958-1990)

This American artist first made a name for himself doing graffiti art on empty advertising boards in the New York City subways. He also did illustrations for children's books.

Jan Vermeer (1632-1675)

Now considered one of the greatest Dutch painters of the 17th century, his work was forgotten for almost 200 years. He left behind fewer than 40 paintings in all.

Jean-Baptiste-Siméon Chardin (1699-1779)

This French artist has been called the greatest still-life painter of his day. He is also known for his quiet portraits of children working and playing.

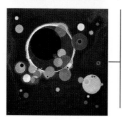

Vasily Kandinsky (1866-1944)

Born in Russia, he originally studied to become a lawyer, but later decided that art was his true calling. He was one of the first artists to make purely abstract paintings.

Émile-Antoine Bourdelle (1861-1929)

This French sculptor was greatly inspired by Gothic and ancient Greek sculpture. He was also a student of Auguste Rodin.

Jasper Johns (1930-   )

By painting everyday objects like flags, numbers, and targets in a loose, expressive style, this American artist bridged the gap between Abstract Expressionism and Pop Art.

Winslow Homer (1836-1910)

This American painter started out as a magazine illustrator. A self-taught artist, he is best known for the seascapes he did later in his life, when he lived on the coast of Maine.

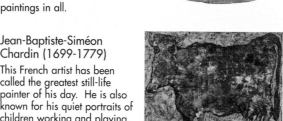

Roy Lichtenstein (1923-1997)

By enlarging images from comic books, including the Benday dots used to print them, this American became one of the biggest names in Pop Art, second only to Andy Warhol.

Claes Oldenburg (1929-   )

Born in Sweden, this Pop sculptor made his mark in America by creating "soft sculptures." These were oversized, stuffed versions of everyday objects such as telephones, toasters. and hamburgers.

Jean Dubuffet (1901-1985)

This French artist worked in a very primitive style. He believed that the art of children and amateurs, which he called Art Brut, or "raw art," was more truthful than that of professional artists.

Henri de Toulouse-Lautrec (1864-1901)

Due to childhood leg injuries, this French artist only grew to be 4½ feet (137 cm) tall. Because he felt isolated by his deformity, he devoted himself completely to sketching and painting scenes from the nightlife of Paris.

Edgar Degas (1834-1917)

Although he is often categorized with the Impressionists, this French painter was more concerned with movement and form than they were. He is best known for his paintings of ballet dancers.

Andy Warhol (1928-1987)

Using the screen printing process, this American artist took images of everyday items, like soup cans, and turned them into art. He called the studio where these images were mass-produced "The Factory."

Jean-Frédéric Bazille (1841-1870)

This French artist, along with his friends Claude Monet, Pierre-Auguste Renoir, and Alfred Sisley, "invented" Impressionism. He was just 29 when he died in the Franco-Prussian War.

Lucio Fontana (1899-1968)

Instead of using paint to create the illusion of space on the canvas, this Italian artist made holes and slashes in the canvas so that real space became part of his work. He was a member of the Spatialism movement.

Théodore Géricault (1791-1824)

This French Romantic painter had an interest in horses and was the student of a well-known horse painter. Ironically, he died at 31 from injuries he suffered falling off a horse.

Vincent van Gogh (1853-1890)

This Dutch painter suffered from mental illness for most of his life and died when he was just 37. In spite of this, he left behind nearly 750 paintings and 1,600 drawings.

Marcus Gheeraerts the Younger (1561/62-1636)

This Flemish painter moved from Belgium to England with his father, Marcus the Elder, when he was six years old. There he eventually became one of the most fashionable portrait painters of his day.

Auguste Rodin (1840-1917)

This French sculptor once created a statue so lifelike, critics thought he had cast it from a live model. He is considered the most important sculptor of the 19th and early 20th centuries.

Paul Klee (1879-1940)

Known for his child-like style, this Swiss-born artist didn't "discover" color until he traveled to Tunisia in 1914. He once said, "A line is a dot that went for a walk."

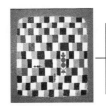

Gerard Dou (1613-1675)

This Dutch painter of everyday life preferred to work on small canvases, and at times he used a magnifying glass to get the details right. He is also known to be the first student of Rembrandt.

Pierre-Auguste Renoir (1841-1919)

Arguably the most popular of all the Impressionist painters, this French artist started out painting designs on china in a porcelain factory.

Frederic Edwin Church (1826-1900)

To capture the beauty and power of nature, this American landscape painter traveled extensively. His paintings show waterfalls, volcanoes, jungles, and icebergs—but no people.

George Caleb Bingham (1811-1879)

Although he was trained as a portrait painter, this American artist is best known for his paintings of frontier life, especially on and around the Missouri River.

Frans Hals (1581-1666)

This Dutch portrait painter's style is very recognizable thanks to his quick, loose brushstrokes. His younger brother Dirck also became a painter, as did five of his eight sons.

Edvard Munch (1863-1944)

One of the founders of a movement called Expressionism, this Norwegian painter exaggerated and distorted his images to show what he was feeling inside.